SUPER EASY SONGBOOK

LEAN ON ME
Songs of Unity, Courage & Hope

ISBN 978-1-70510-545-0

HAL•LEONARD®

Visit Hal Leonard Online at
www.halleonard.com

Contact us:
Hal Leonard
7777 West Bluemound Road
Milwaukee, WI 53213
Email: info@halleonard.com

In Europe, contact:
Hal Leonard Europe Limited
42 Wigmore Street
Marylebone, London, W1U 2RN
Email: info@halleonardeurope.com

In Australia, contact:
Hal Leonard Australia Pty. Ltd.
4 Lentara Court
Cheltenham, Victoria, 3192 Australia
Email: info@halleonard.com.au

Welcome to the *Super Easy Songbook* series!

This unique collection will help you play your favorite songs quickly and easily. Here's how it works:

- Play the simplified melody with your right hand. Letter names appear inside each note to assist you.

- There are no key signatures to worry about! If a sharp ♯ or flat ♭ is needed, it is shown beside the note each time.

- There are no page turns, so your hands never have to leave the keyboard.

- If two notes are connected by a tie ⌣, hold the first note for the combined number of beats. (The second note does not show a letter name since it is not re-struck.)

- Add basic chords with your left hand using the provided keyboard diagrams. Chord voicings have been carefully chosen to minimize hand movement.

- The left-hand rhythm is up to you, and chord notes can be played together or separately. Be creative!

- If the chords sound muddy, move your left hand an octave* higher. If this gets in the way of playing the melody, move your right hand an octave higher as well.

   An octave spans eight notes. If your starting note is C, the next C to the right is an octave higher.

———————————————— ALSO AVAILABLE ————————————————

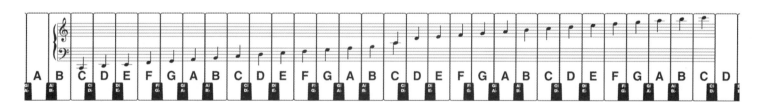

Hal Leonard Student Keyboard Guide HL00296039

Key Stickers HL00100016

At the Same Time

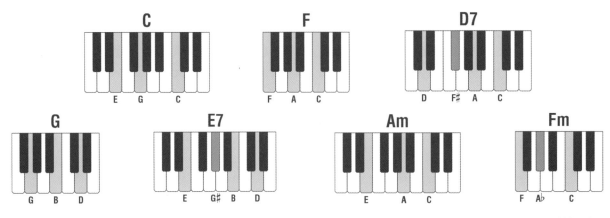

Words and Music by
Ann Hampton Callaway

Moderately slow

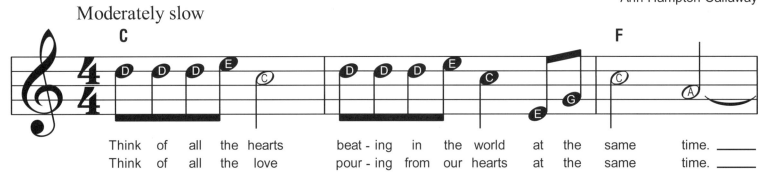

Think of all the hearts beat - ing in the world at the same time. _____
Think of all the love pour - ing from our hearts at the same time. _____

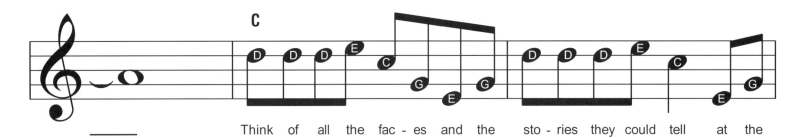

_____ Think of all the fac - es and the sto - ries they could tell at the
_____ Think of all the light our love can shine a - round this world at the

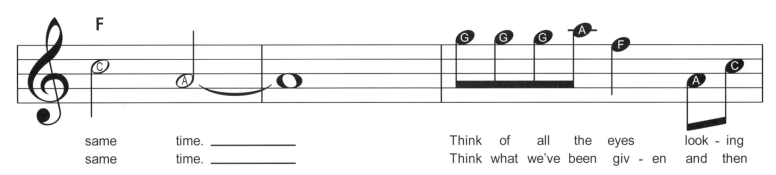

same time. _____ Think of all the eyes look - ing
same time. _____ Think what we've been giv - en and then

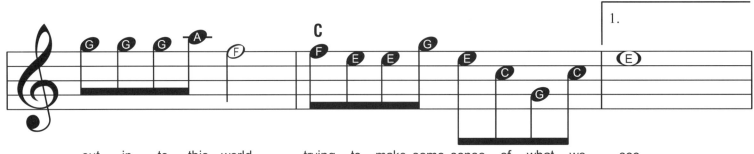

out in - to this world, trying to make some sense of what we see.
think what we could lose. All of life is in our trem - bling

Better Days

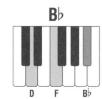
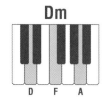
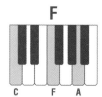

Words and Music by Ryan Tedder,
Brent Kutzle and John Nathaniel

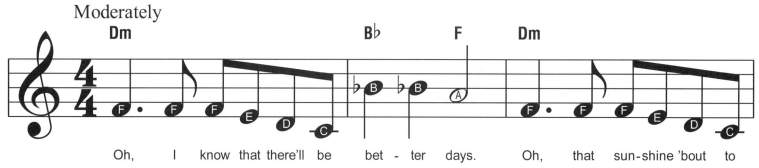

Oh, I know that there'll be bet-ter days. Oh, that sun-shine 'bout to

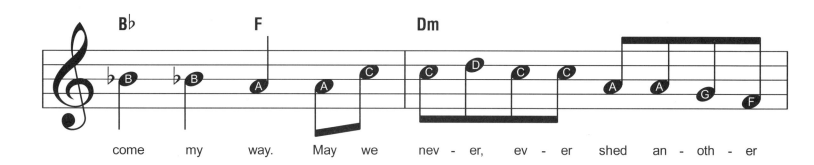

come my way. May we nev-er, ev-er shed an-oth-er

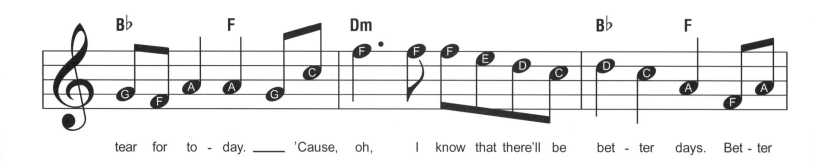

tear for to-day. ____ 'Cause, oh, I know that there'll be bet-ter days. Bet-ter

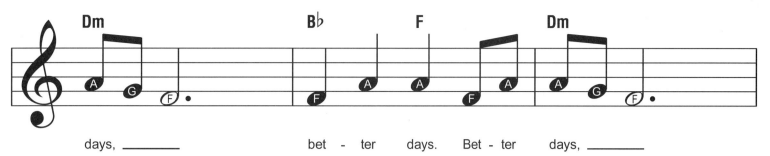

days, _____ bet - ter days. Bet - ter days, _____

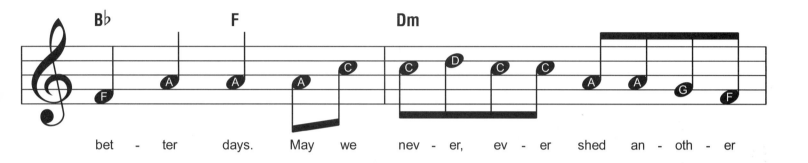

bet - ter days. May we nev - er, ev - er shed an - oth - er

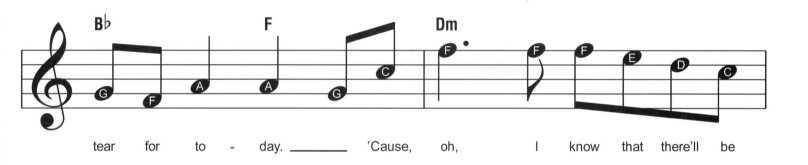

tear for to - day. _____ 'Cause, oh, I know that there'll be

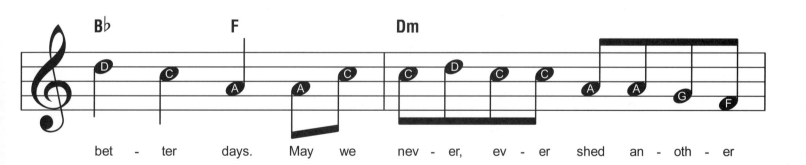

bet - ter days. May we nev - er, ev - er shed an - oth - er

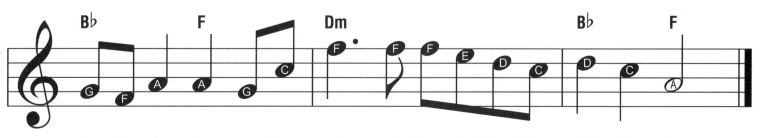

tear for to - day. ____ 'Cause, oh, I know that there'll be bet - ter days.

Count on Me

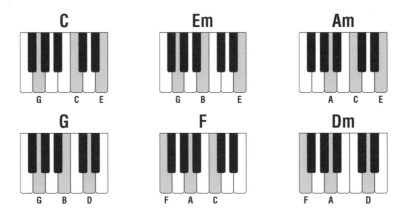

Words and Music by Bruno Mars,
Ari Levine and Philip Lawrence

Ebony and Ivory

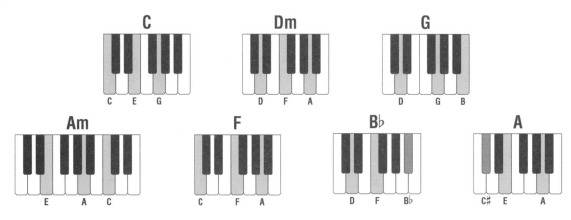

Words and Music by
Paul McCartney

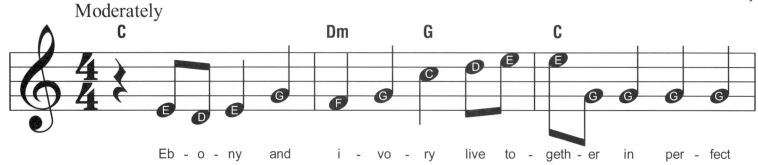

Eb - o - ny and i - vo - ry live to - geth - er in per - fect

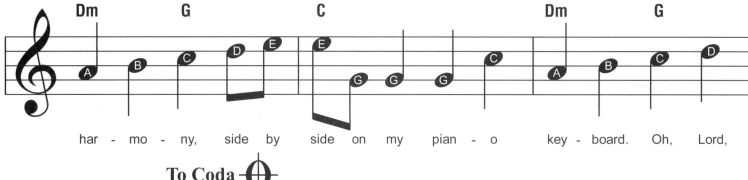

har - mo - ny, side by side on my pian - o key - board. Oh, Lord,

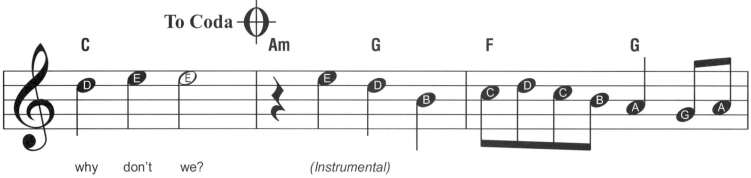

why don't we?   (Instrumental)

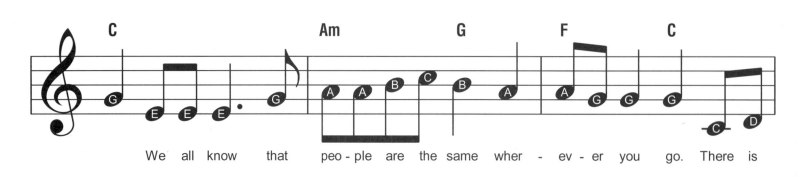

We all know that peo - ple are the same wher - ev - er you go. There is

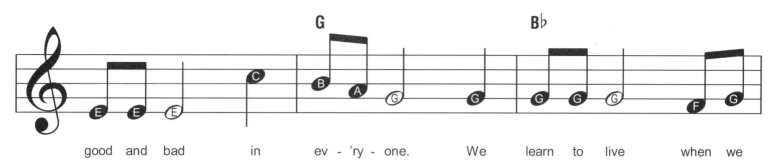

good and bad   in ev - 'ry - one.   We   learn   to   live   when   we

D.C. al Coda
(Return to beginning,
play to ✛ and skip to Coda)

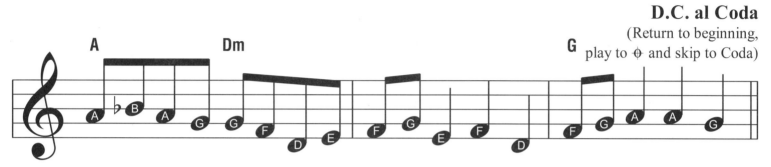

learn   to give each oth - er   what   we   need   to sur - vive, to - geth - er   a - live. ____

CODA

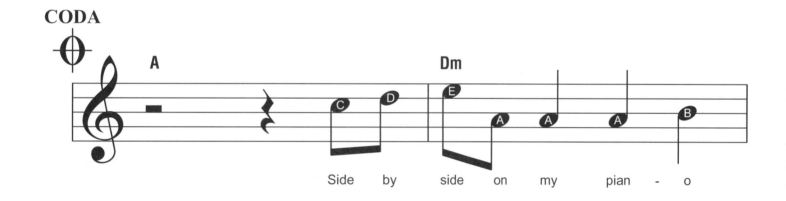

Side   by   side   on   my   pian - o

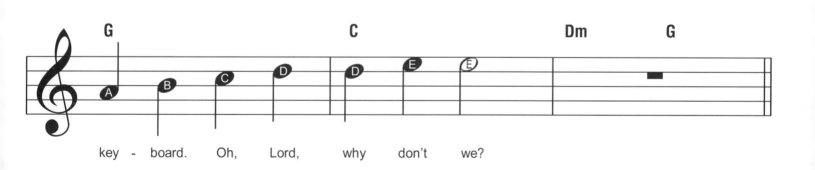

key - board.   Oh,   Lord,   why   don't   we?

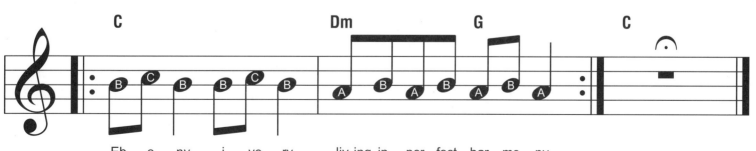

Eb - o - ny,   i - vo - ry,   liv-ing in per - fect har - mo - ny.

11

Fight Song

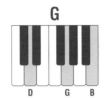
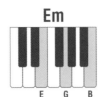
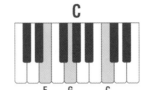
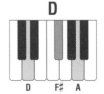

Words and Music by Rachel Platten
and Dave Bassett

With confidence

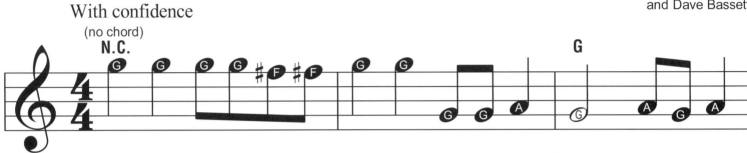

(Instrumental)

Like a small boat on the o-

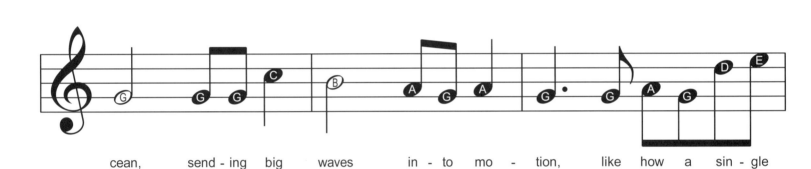

cean, send-ing big waves in-to mo-tion, like how a sin-gle

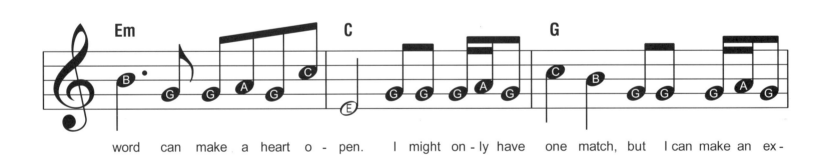

word can make a heart o-pen. I might on-ly have one match, but I can make an ex-

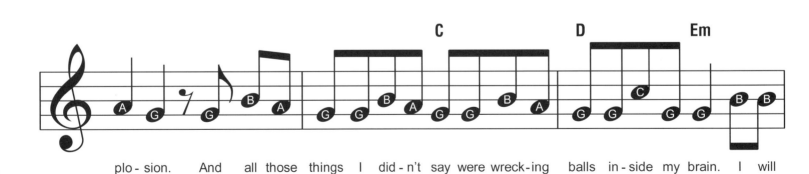

plo-sion. And all those things I did-n't say were wreck-ing balls in-side my brain. I will

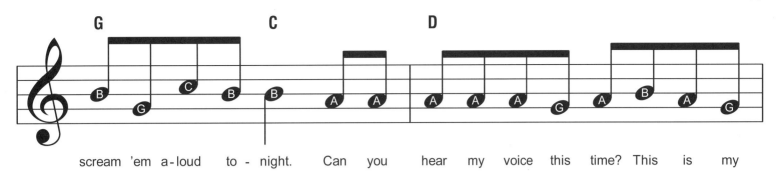

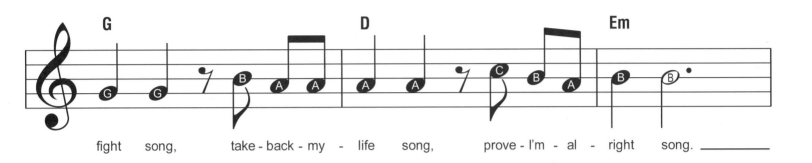

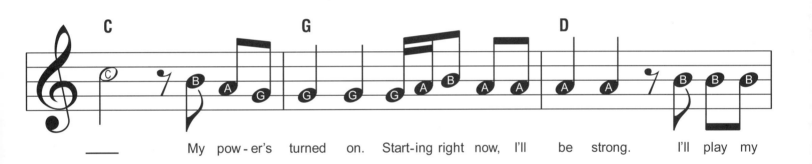

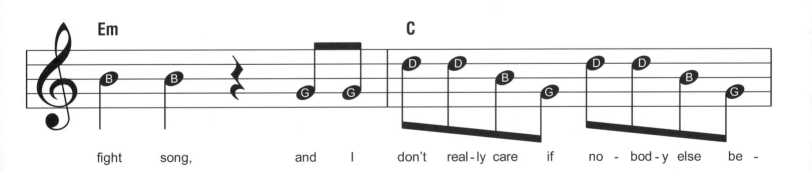

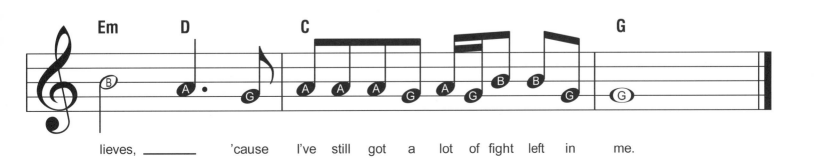

From a Distance

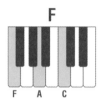
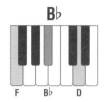
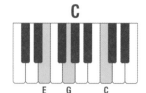
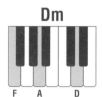

Words and Music by
Julie Gold

Moderately slow

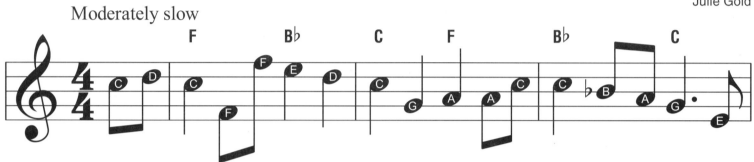

From a dis-tance, the world looks blue and green, and the snow-capped _ moun-tains

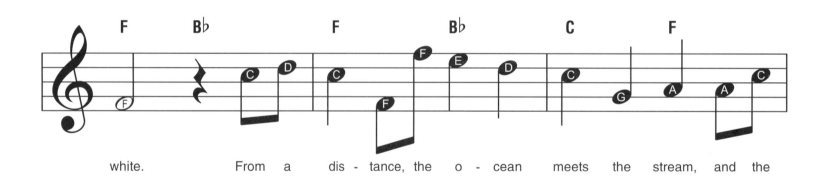

white. From a dis-tance, the o-cean meets the stream, and the

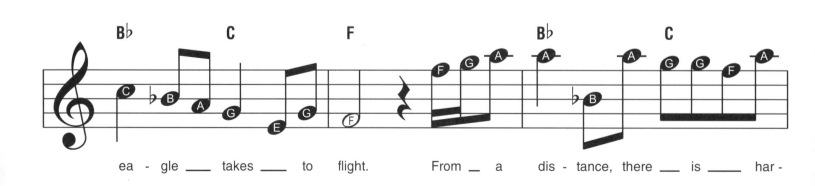

ea-gle ___ takes ___ to flight. From _ a dis-tance, there ___ is ___ har-

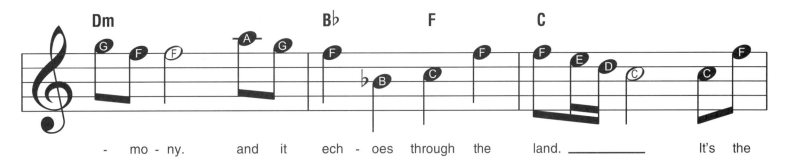

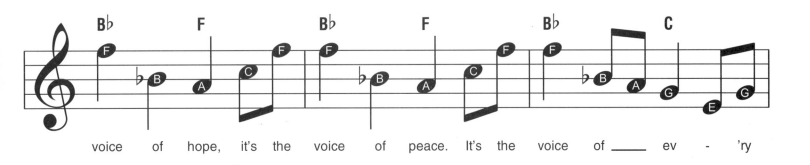

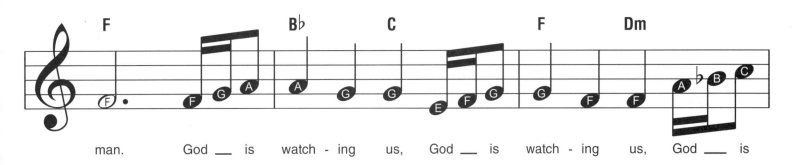

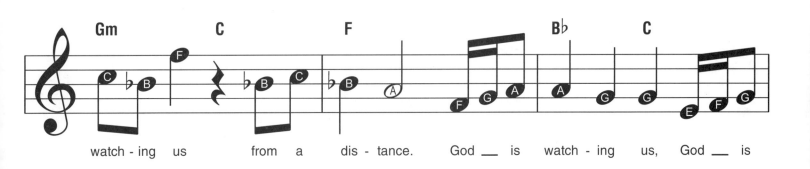

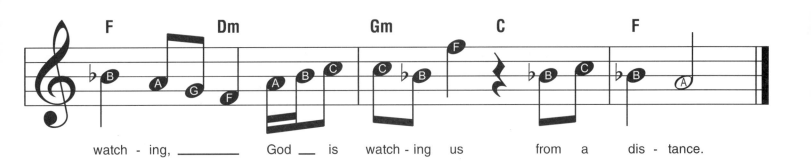

Heal the World

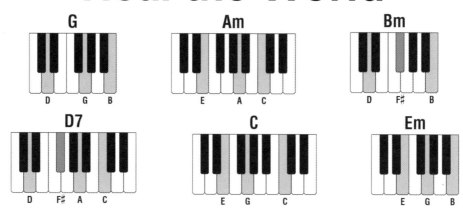

Words and Music by
Michael Jackson

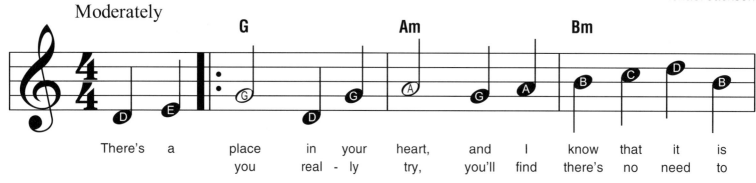

There's a place in your heart, and I know that it is
you real - ly try, you'll find there's no need to

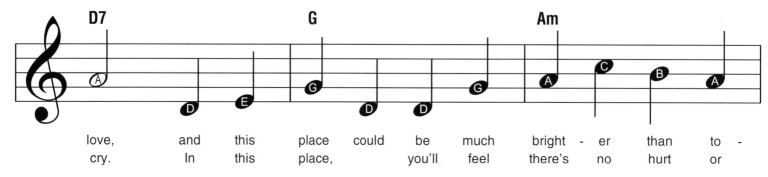

love, and this place could be much bright - er than to -
cry. In this this place, you'll much feel there's no hurt or

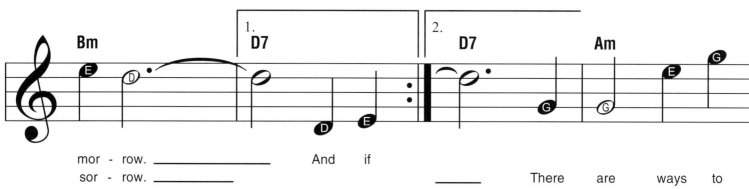

mor - row. _____ And if
sor - row. _____ There are ways to

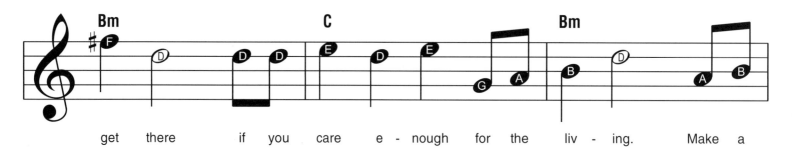

get there if you care e - nough for the liv - ing. Make a

Home

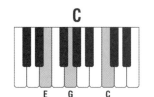
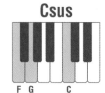
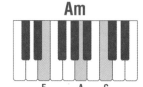
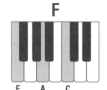
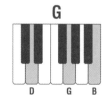

Words and Music by Greg Holden
and Drew Pearson

Brightly

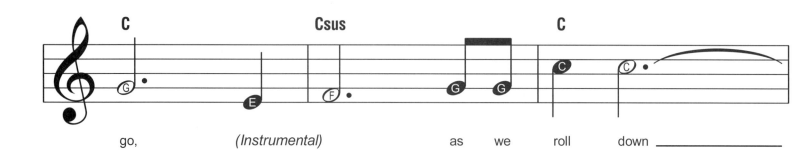

Hold on _____ to me as we

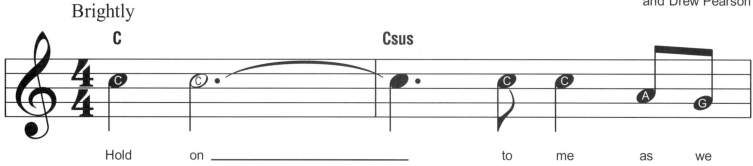

go, (Instrumental) as we roll down _____

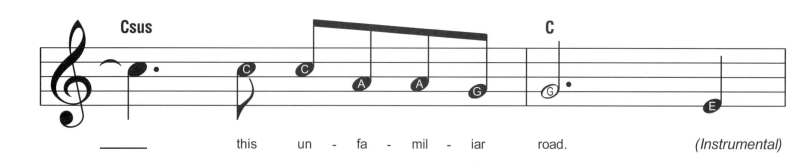

____ this un-fa-mil-iar road. (Instrumental)

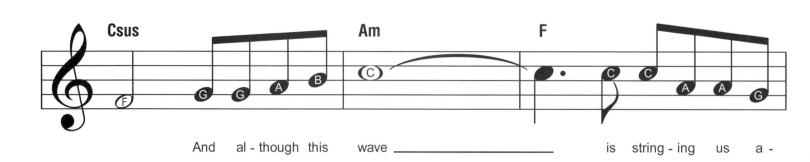

And al-though this wave _____ is string-ing us a-

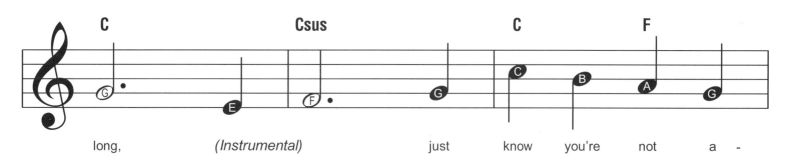

long,   *(Instrumental)*   just   know   you're   not   a -

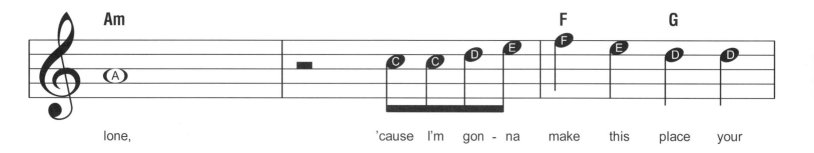

lone,   'cause   I'm   gon - na   make   this   place   your

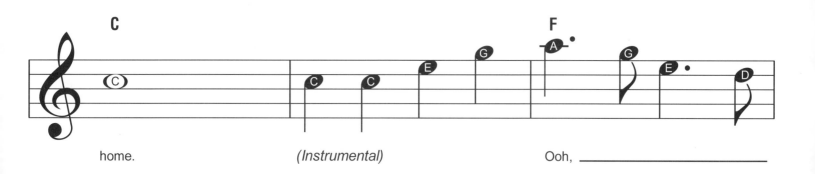

home.   *(Instrumental)*   Ooh, _____

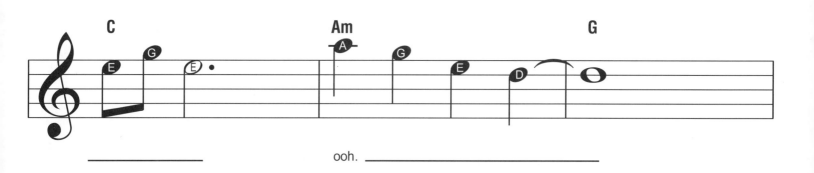

_____   ooh. _____

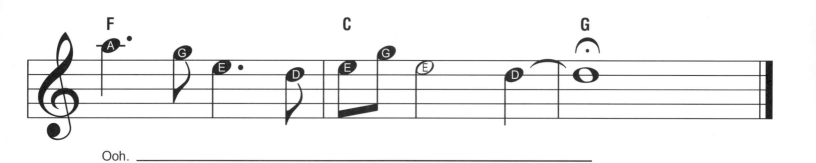

Ooh. _____

I Dare You

 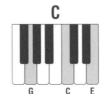 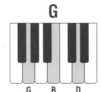

Words and Music by Benjamin West,
Jeffrey Gitelman, Natalie Hemby,
Laura Veltz and Jesse Shatkin

Moderately

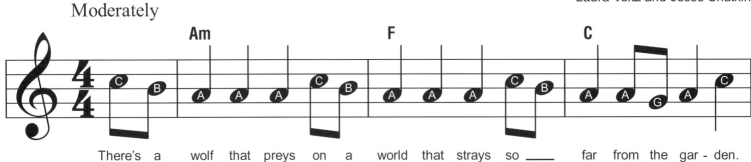

There's a wolf that preys on a world that strays so ___ far from the gar-den.

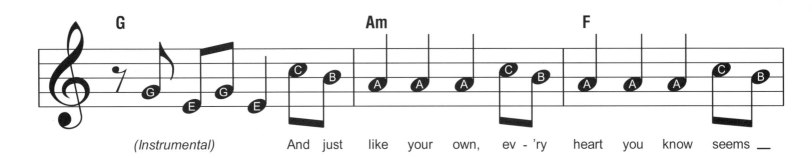

(Instrumental) And just like your own, ev-'ry heart you know seems ___

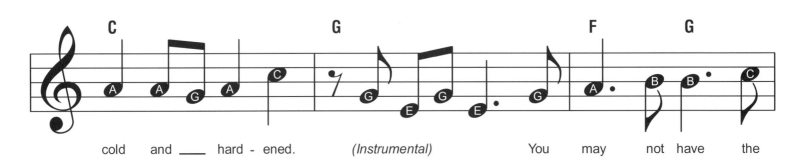

cold and ___ hard-ened. *(Instrumental)* You may not have the

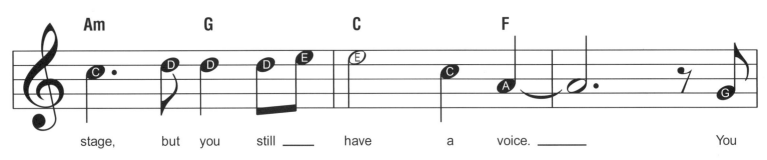

stage, but you still ___ have a voice. ___ You

Lean on Me

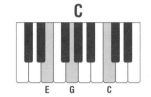
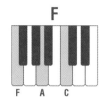

Words and Music by
Bill Withers

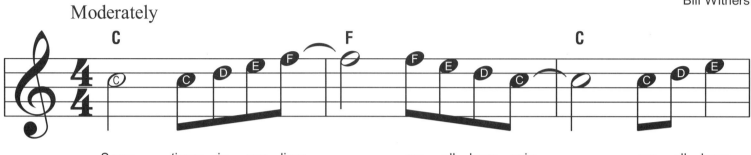

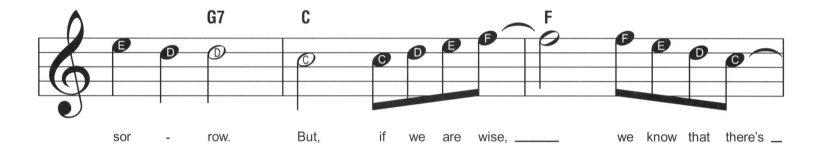

Some - times in our lives, _____ we all have pain, _____ we all have

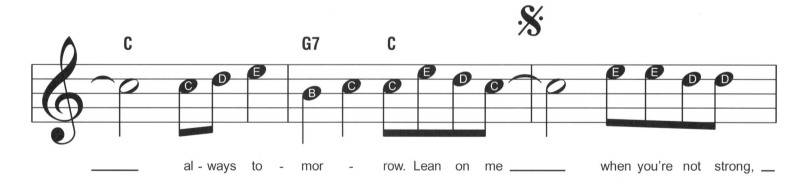

sor - row. But, if we are wise, _____ we know that there's _

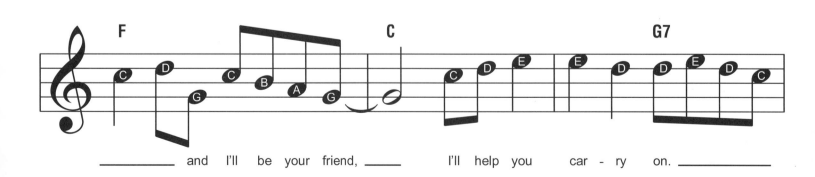

_____ al - ways to - mor - row. Lean on me _____ when you're not strong, _

_____ and I'll be your friend, _____ I'll help you car - ry on. _____

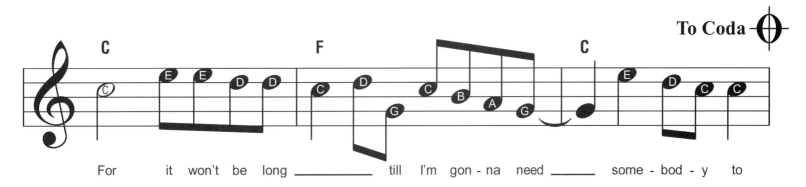

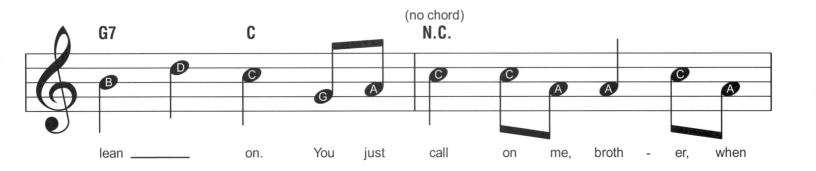

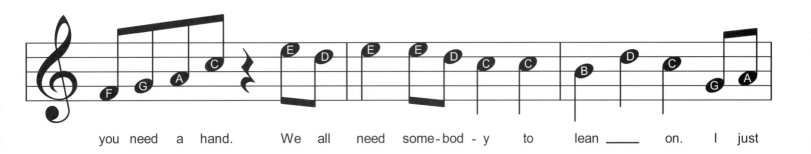

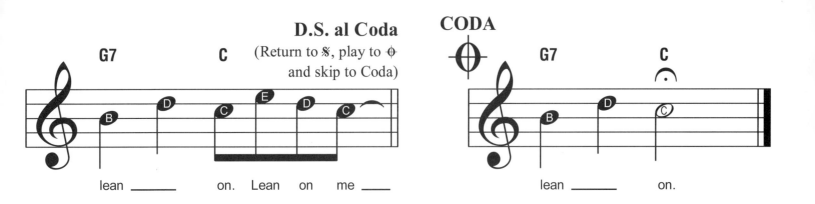

This page has been intentionally left blank
to avoid unnecessary page turns.

Love Wins

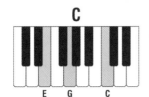 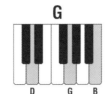 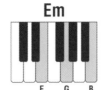 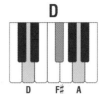

Words and Music by David Garcia,
Brett James and Carrie Underwood

One Call Away

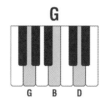
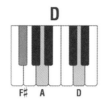
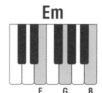
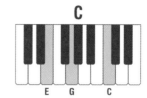

Words and Music by Charlie Puth,
Justin Franks, Breyan Isaac,
Matt Prime, Blake Anthony Carter
and Maureen McDonald

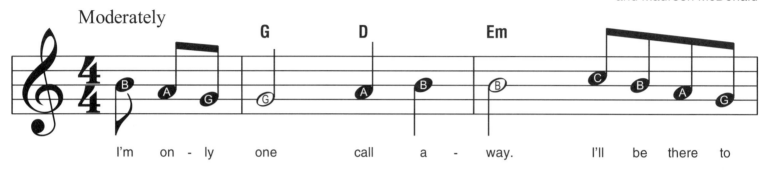

I'm on-ly one call a-way. I'll be there to

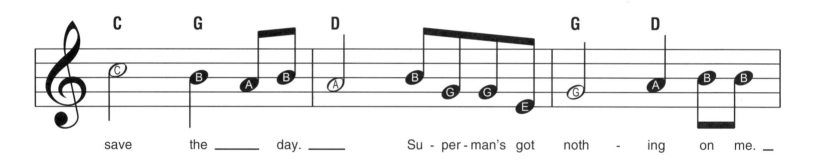

save the ___ day. ___ Su-per-man's got noth - ing on me. ___

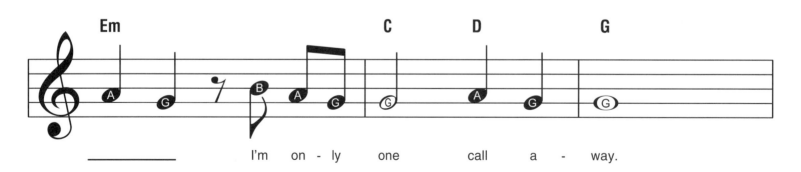

___ I'm on-ly one call a-way.

Rise Up

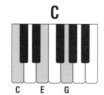
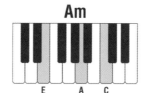
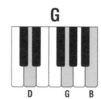
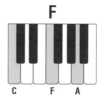

Words and Music by Cassandra Batie
and Jennifer Decilveo

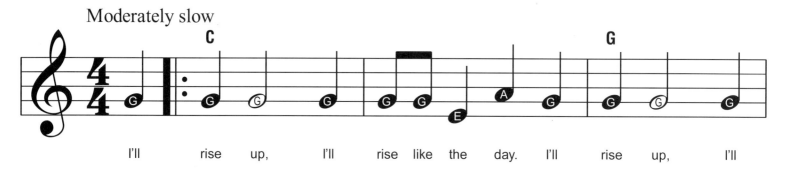

I'll rise up, I'll rise like the day. I'll rise up, I'll

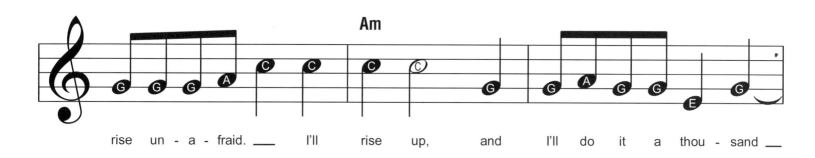

rise un - a - fraid. ___ I'll rise up, and I'll do it a thou - sand ___

___ times a - gain. And I'll rise up, I'll

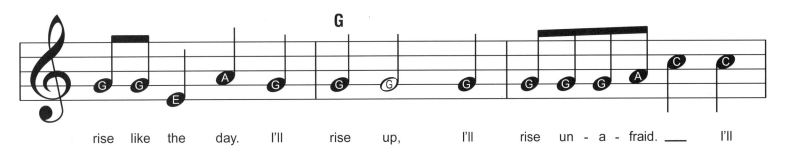

rise like the day. I'll rise up, I'll rise un - a - fraid. ___ I'll

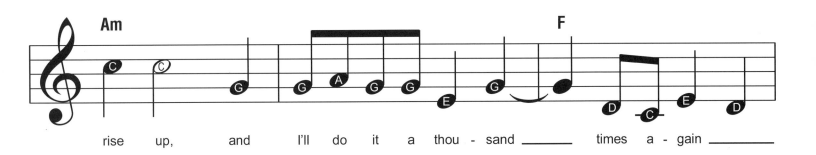

rise up, and I'll do it a thou - sand _____ times a - gain _____

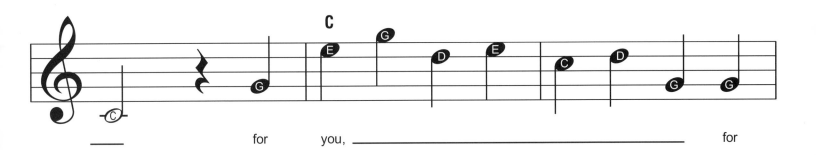

___ for you, _____ for

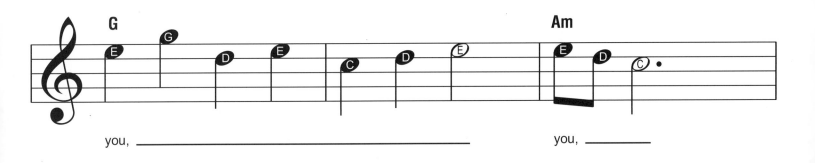

you, _____ you, _____

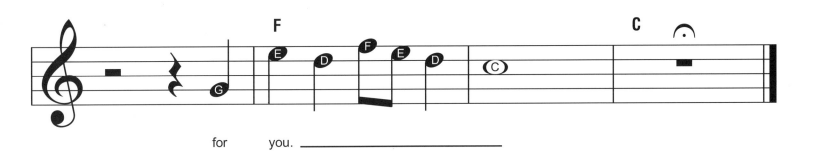

for you. _____

Stand by Me

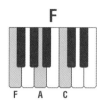
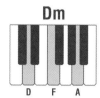
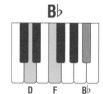
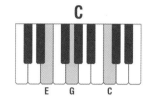

Words and Music by Jerry Leiber,
Mike Stoller and Ben E. King

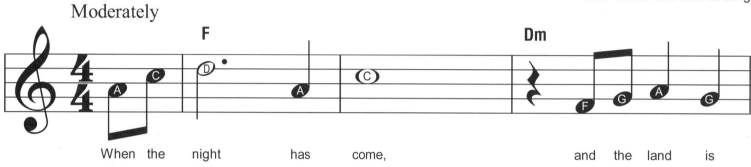

When the night has come, and the land is

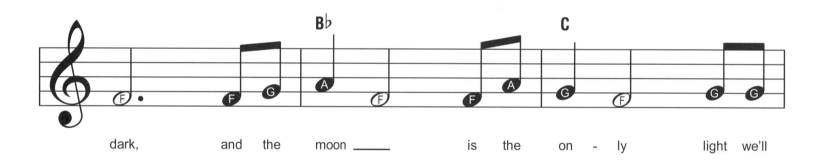

dark, and the moon _____ is the on - ly light we'll

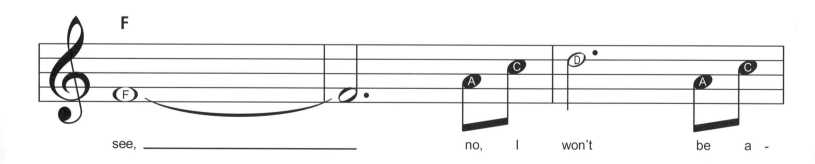

see, _____ no, I won't be a -

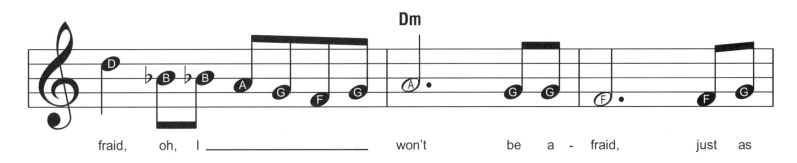

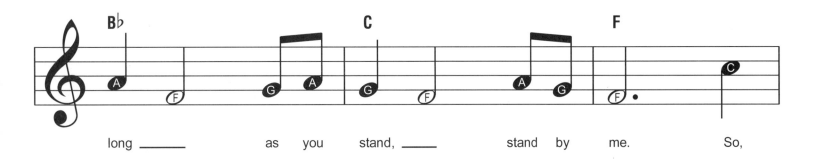

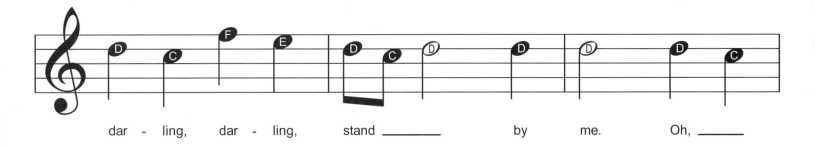

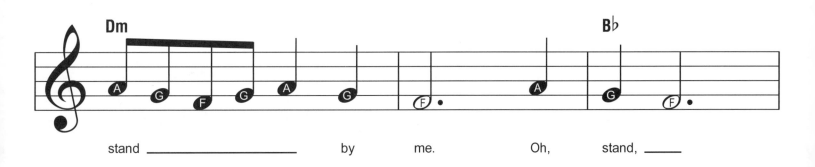

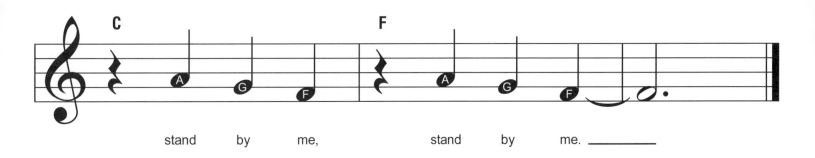

Tomorrow
from the Musical Production ANNIE

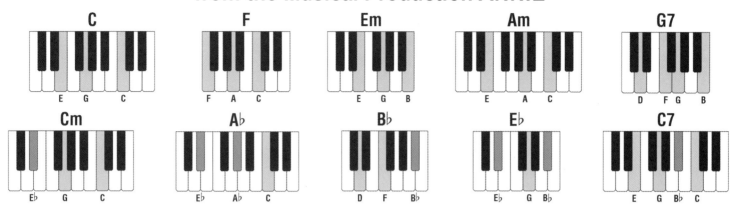

Lyric by Martin Charnin
Music by Charles Strouse

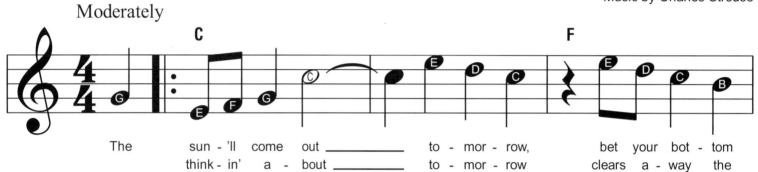

The sun-'ll come out _____ to-mor-row, bet your bot-tom
think-in' a-bout _____ to-mor-row clears a-way the

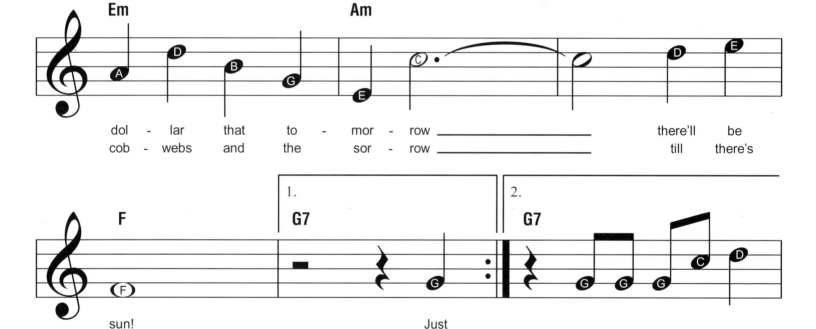

dol-lar that to-mor-row _____ there'll be
cob-webs and the sor-row _____ till there's

sun! Just
none. When I'm stuck with a

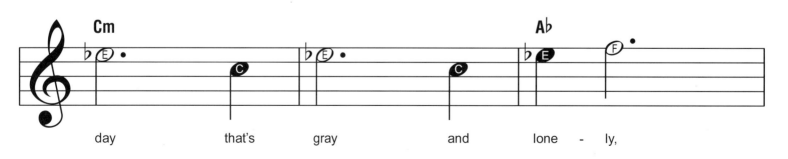

day that's gray and lone-ly,

Underdog

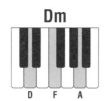
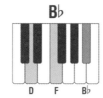
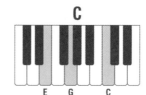
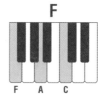

Words and Music by Alicia Augello-Cook,
Ed Sheeran, Amy Wadge,
Foy Vance, Jonny Coffer
and Johnny McDaid

Moderate Shuffle

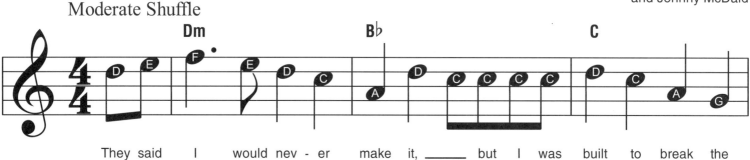

They said I would nev-er make it, _____ but I was built to break the

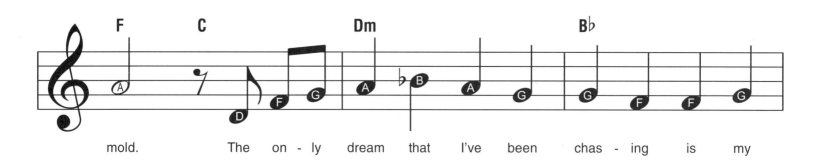

mold. The on-ly dream that I've been chas-ing is my

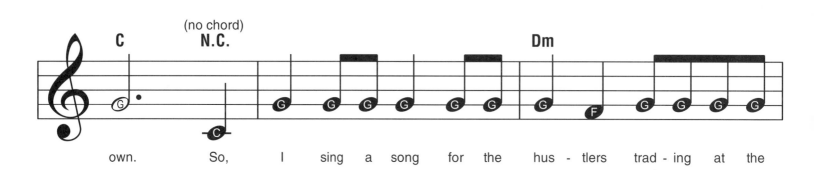

own. So, I sing a song for the hus-tlers trad-ing at the

35

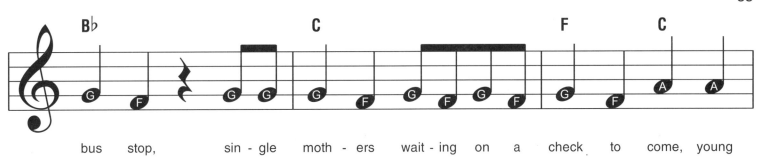

bus stop, sin - gle moth - ers wait - ing on a check to come, young

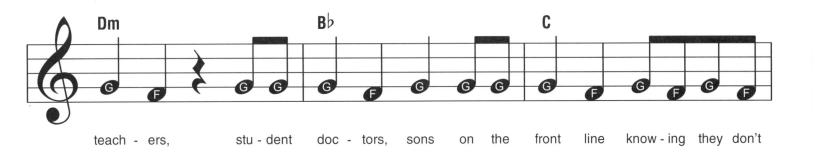

teach - ers, stu - dent doc - tors, sons on the front line know - ing they don't

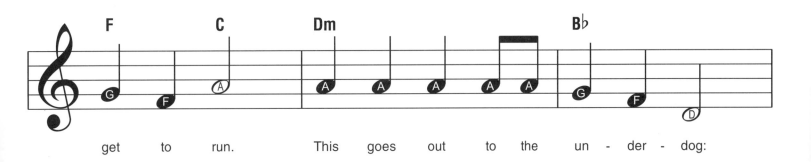

get to run. This goes out to the un - der - dog:

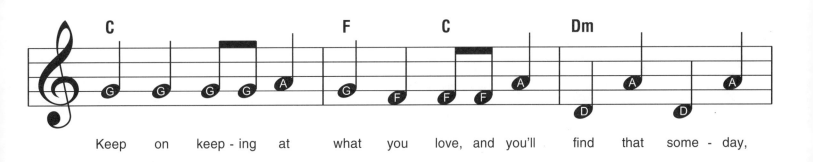

Keep on keep - ing at what you love, and you'll find that some - day,

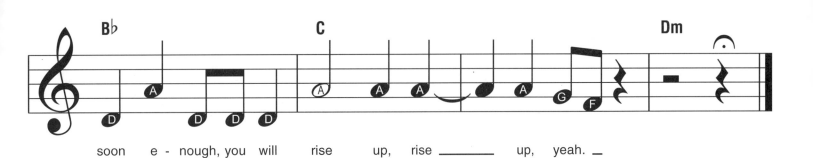

soon e - nough, you will rise up, rise _____ up, yeah. _

We Are Warriors
(Warrior)

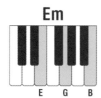
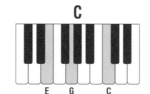
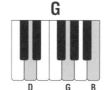
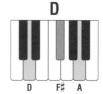

Words and Music by Avril Lavigne,
Chad Kroeger and Travis Clark

We're All in This Together
from HIGH SCHOOL MUSICAL

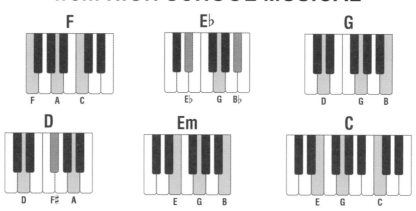

Words and Music by Matthew Gerrard
and Robbie Nevil

With energy

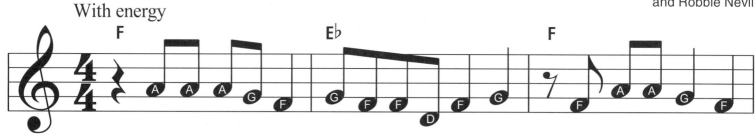

Here and now, __ it's time for cel - e - bra - tion. I fi - n'lly fig - ured

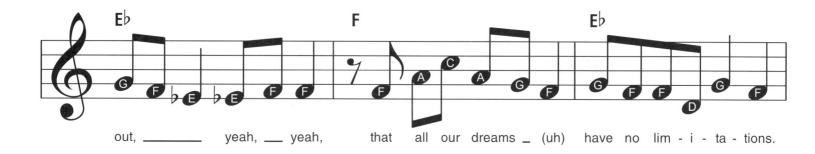

out, _____ yeah, __ yeah, that all our dreams _ (uh) have no lim - i - ta - tions.

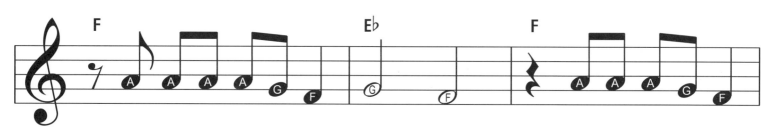

That's what it's all ____ a - bout. _____ Ev - 'ry - one ____ is

spe - cial in their own way. We make each oth - er strong.

With a Little Help from My Friends

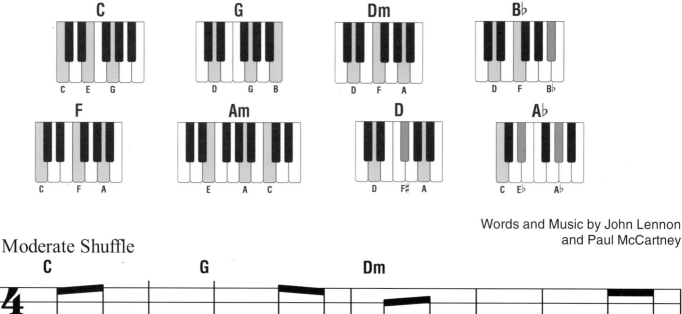

Words and Music by John Lennon
and Paul McCartney

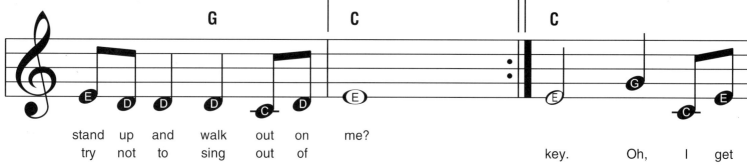

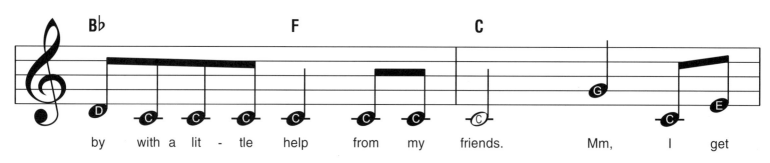

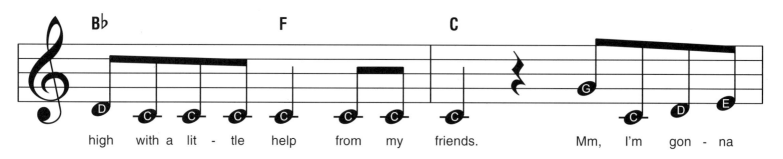

You Will Be Found

from DEAR EVAN HANSEN

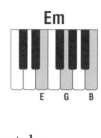
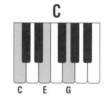
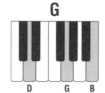
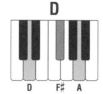

Music and Lyrics by Benj Pasek
and Justin Paul

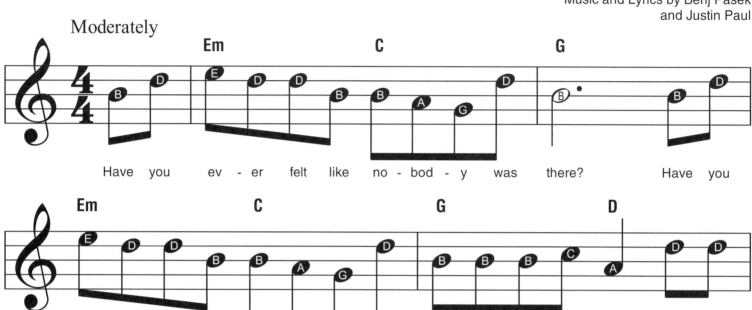

Have you ev - er felt like no - bod - y was there? Have you
ev - er felt for - got - ten in the mid - dle of no - where? Have you

ev - er felt like you could dis - ap - pear? Like you could fall, and no one would

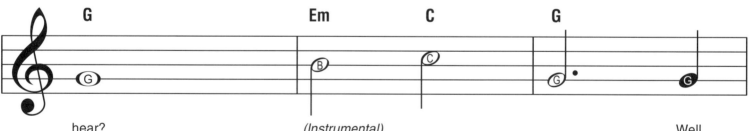

hear? (Instrumental) Well,

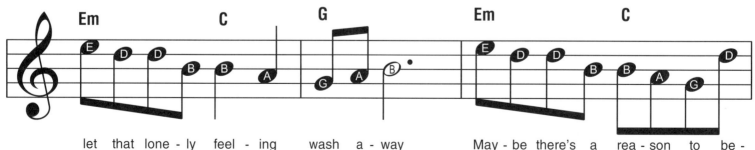

let that lone - ly feel - ing wash a - way May - be there's a rea - son to be -

You'll Never Walk Alone

from CAROUSEL

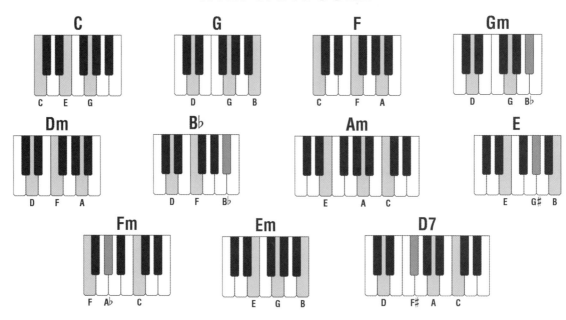

Lyrics by Oscar Hammerstein II
Music by Richard Rodgers

Moderately

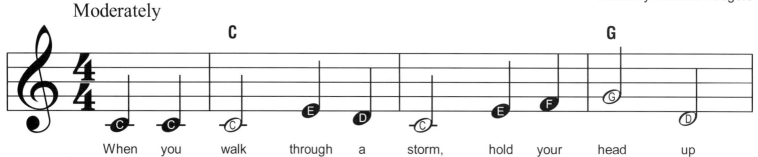

When you walk through a storm, hold your head up

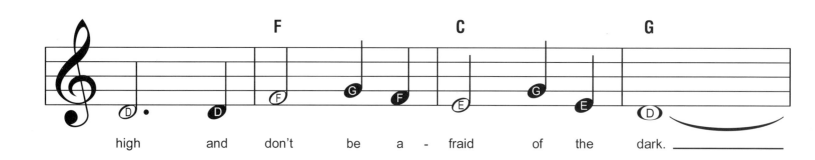

high and don't be a - fraid of the dark. _____

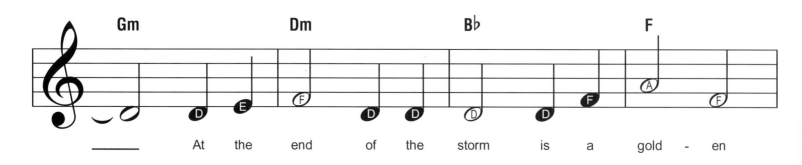

_____ At the end of the storm is a gold - en

45

You've Got a Friend

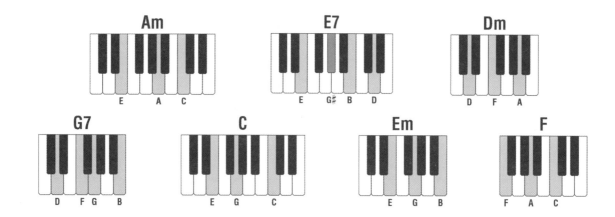

Words and Music by
Carole King

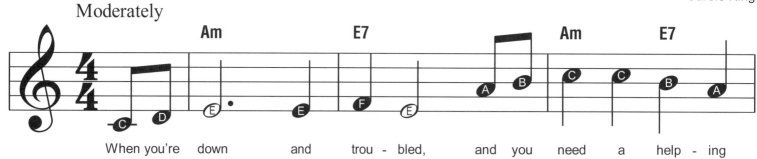

When you're down and trou-bled, and you need a help-ing

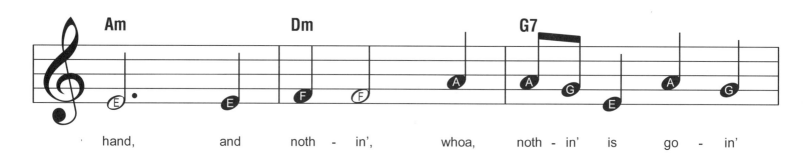

hand, and noth-in', whoa, noth-in' is go-in'

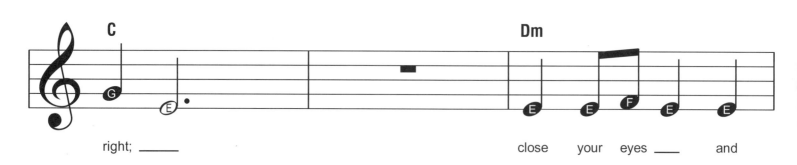

right; _____ close your eyes _____ and

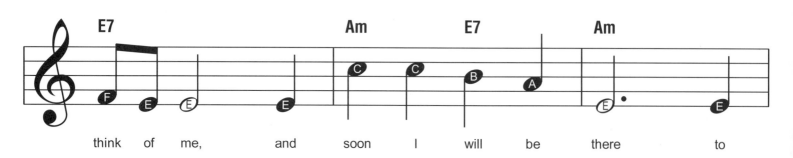

think of me, and soon I will be there to

SUPER EASY SONGBOOK

It's super easy! This series features accessible arrangements for piano, with simple right-hand melody, letter names inside each note, and basic left-hand chord diagrams. Perfect for players of all ages!

THE BEATLES
00198161 60 songs $15.99

BEAUTIFUL BALLADS
00385162 50 songs $14.99

BEETHOVEN
00345533 21 selections $9.99

BEST SONGS EVER
00329877 60 songs $16.99

BROADWAY
00193871 60 songs $15.99

JOHNNY CASH
00287524 20 songs $9.99

CHART HITS
00380277 24 songs $12.99

CHRISTMAS CAROLS
00277955 60 songs $15.99

CHRISTMAS SONGS
00236850 60 songs $15.99

**CHRISTMAS SONGS
WITH 3 CHORDS**
00367423 30 songs $10.99

CLASSIC ROCK
00287526 60 songs $15.99

CLASSICAL
00194693 60 selections $15.99

COUNTRY
00285257 60 songs $15.99

DISNEY
00199558 60 songs $15.99

BOB DYLAN
00364487 22 songs $12.99

BILLIE EILISH
00346515 22 songs $10.99

FOLKSONGS
00381031 60 songs $15.99

FOUR CHORD SONGS
00249533 60 songs $15.99

FROZEN COLLECTION
00334069 14 songs $10.99

GEORGE GERSHWIN
00345536 22 songs $9.99

GOSPEL
00285256 60 songs $15.99

HIT SONGS
00194367 60 songs $16.99

HYMNS
00194659 60 songs $15.99

JAZZ STANDARDS
00233687 60 songs $15.99

BILLY JOEL
00329996 22 songs $10.99

ELTON JOHN
00298762 22 songs $10.99

KIDS' SONGS
00198009 60 songs $15.99

LEAN ON ME
00350593 22 songs $9.99

THE LION KING
00303511 9 songs $9.99

ANDREW LLOYD WEBBER
00249580 48 songs $19.99

MOVIE SONGS
00233670 60 songs $15.99

PEACEFUL MELODIES
00367880 60 songs $16.99

POP SONGS FOR KIDS
00346809 60 songs $16.99

POP STANDARDS
00233770 60 songs $16.99

QUEEN
00294889 20 songs $10.99

ED SHEERAN
00287525 20 songs $9.99

SIMPLE SONGS
00329906 60 songs $15.99

**STAR WARS
(EPISODES I-IX)**
00345560 17 songs $10.99

TAYLOR SWIFT
1192568 30 songs $14.99

THREE CHORD SONGS
00249664 60 songs $15.99

TOP HITS
00300405 22 songs $10.99

WORSHIP
00294871 60 songs $15.99

HAL•LEONARD®
www.halleonard.com

0223